Contents

KT-116-351

Some words are shown in bold, **like this**.
You can find them in the glossary on page 23.

Have you seen the sky?

When you are outside, if you look up you will see the sky.

The sky is always above you at the beach or the city.

What is the Sky?

Monica Hughes

Raintree

www.raintreepublishers.co.uk

Visit our website to find out more information about **Raintree** books.

To order:
☎ Phone 44 (0) 1865 888112
🖨 Send a fax to 44 (0) 1865 314091
💻 Visit the Raintree Bookshop at **www.raintreepublishers.co.uk** to browse our catalogue and order online.

First published in Great Britain by Raintree, Halley Court, Jordan Hill, Oxford OX2 8EJ, part of Harcourt Education.
Raintree is a registered trademark of Harcourt Education Ltd.

© Harcourt Education Ltd 2005
First published in paperback in 2006
The moral right of the proprietor has been asserted.

All rights reserved. No part of this publication may be reproduced, stored in a retrieval system, or transmitted in any form or by any means, electronic, mechanical, photocopying, recording, or otherwise, without either the prior written permission of the publishers or a licence permitting restricted copying in the United Kingdom issued by the Copyright Licensing Agency Ltd, 90 Tottenham Court Road, London W1T 4LP (www.cla.co.uk).

Editorial: Catherine Clarke and Sarah Chappelow
Design: Michelle Lisseter
Picture Research: Maria Joannou, Erica Newbery and Kay Altwegg
Production: Amanda Meaden

Originated by Dot Gradations Ltd
Printed and bound in China by South China Printing Company

ISBN 1 844 43648 9(hardback)
09 08 07 06 05
10 9 8 7 6 5 4 3 2 1

ISBN 1 844 43654 3(paperback)
10 09 08 07 06
10 9 8 7 6 5 4 3 2 1

British Library Cataloguing in Publication Data
Hughes, Monica
What is the Sky?. – (The World Around Us)
551.5
A full catalogue record for this book is available from the British Library.

Acknowledgements
The publishers would like to thank the following for permission to reproduce photographs: Alamy pp. **7** (John Foxx), **13** (Peter Usbeck), **15** (Image Farm Inc); **21** (Brand X Pictures), **23c** (Peter Usbeck); Corbis (B.S.P.I.) pp. **16**, **22**; Getty Images (Photodisc) pp. **6**, **17**, **22**, **23a**; Harcourt Education Ltd (Corbis) pp. **4**, **8**, **10**, **11**, **14**, **18**, **19**, **20**, **22**, **23d**, **23e**; KPT Power Photos pp. **12**, **23b**; Science Photo Library (David Nunuk) pp. **5**, **9**.

Cover photograph reproduced with permission of Corbis.

Every effort has been made to contact copyright holders of any material reproduced in this book. Any omissions will be rectified in subsequent printings if notice is given to the publishers.

The paper used to print this book comes from sustainable resources.

All over the world the sky is above you.

The sky does not always look the same, though.

What is the sky like in the day?

The Sun lights up the sky during the day.

Sometimes the sky is bright blue and there are no **clouds**.

Sometimes the sky looks white, or even grey.

There is less light because the clouds cover the Sun.

What is the sky like at night?

If there are no **clouds** at night you can see the **Moon**.

The Moon does not always look the same shape.

The sky is darker at night because the Sun cannot be seen.

Sometimes you can see the light from bright stars.

When does the sky change colour?

Every morning the Sun rises and lights up the sky.

The sky may look red, yellow, or even orange at **sunrise**.

At the end of the day the Sun goes down and night begins.

The sky changes colour again as the Sun sets.

How does the sky show the weather?

Looking at the sky can tell you what the weather will be.

Clear blue skies and thin **clouds** mean a warm, dry day.

Dark grey or black clouds often bring rain.

Lightning lights up the sky during a thunderstorm.

What falls from the sky?

Rain falls from grey or black **clouds** in the sky.

After rain, the clouds in the sky are white.

When it is very cold, snow falls from clouds instead of rain.

Snow can be blown across the sky by strong winds.

How big is the sky?

The sky is made of air called the **atmosphere**.

When you look up at air balloons, you only see part of the sky.

The sky stretches away from the Earth into space.

We look through the atmosphere to see the Sun, **Moon** and stars.

How do animals and plants use sky?

Animals need air to breathe and light and warmth from the Sun.

Birds and insects use the sky to fly about.

Plants need rain from the sky
to grow.

Many plants grow upwards and
turn to face the Sun in the sky.

How do people use the sky?

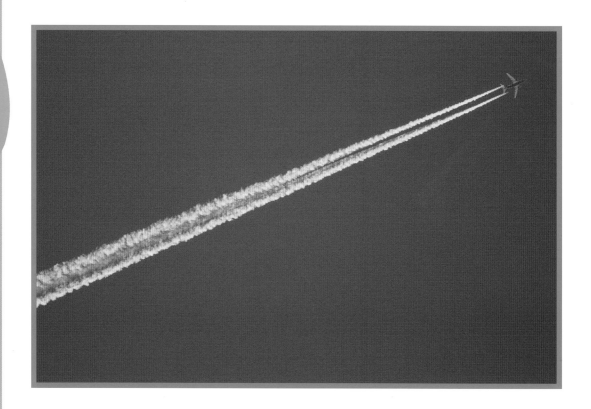

People need air to breathe, just like animals and plants.

We can use the sky to travel from place to place in aeroplanes.

People also use the sky to have fun.

There are lots of different ways to enjoy the sky!

Quiz

Which of these types of transport use the sky?

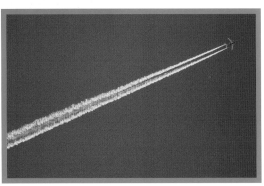

Glossary

atmosphere
air or gases surrounding the Earth

cloud
white, grey, or black patches in the sky. Rain and snow fall from clouds.

lightning
natural electricity made during a storm. Lightning makes a bright flash of light.

Moon
huge object that moves around Earth and can usually be seen in the sky at night

sunrise
time of day when the Sun comes up and first appears in the sky

Index

Answer to quiz on page 22

Aeroplanes and air balloons use the sky.